The Real Scientist
Stuff!
Materials and how they change

W

FRANKLIN WATTS
LONDON•SYDNEY

Contents

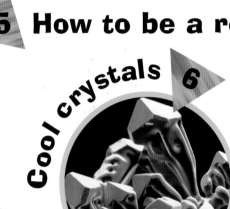 

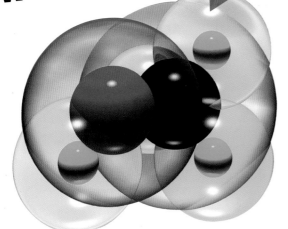

Amazing materials

Our world is full of stuff – just look around you. It's *everywhere*! You might be thinking of the objects you can see, such as this book or a table. But what about the stuff the object is made of? Real scientists call this type of stuff a material. There are thousands of different materials, each made from a different kind of matter – a solid, liquid or gas.

Some kinds of matter can change their form. Just think about water. It is normally a liquid but it can be frozen into a solid, called ice, or boiled into a gas, called steam.

▶ Solids, such as these sugar cubes, have a fixed shape and volume.

◀ Liquids, like syrup, have a fixed volume but they change their shape as you pour them from one container to another.

▶ Gases, such as those in a balloon, have no fixed size or shape. They fill up the space available.

▲ When some kinds of stuff get together they make new stuff. For example, if you mix cornflour and water you get a sticky goo.

How to be a real scientist

Real scientists look at our world and try to understand it by thinking about it and performing experiments. You can be a real scientist too! Just look at each topic, read the 'getting going' section and then get experimenting.

Set up a science box

Find a large box, then skip through the pages in this book and look at the things you need for each activity. Collect them up and put them in your science box.

Use these science skills

▶ **Observe**
Look carefully at whatever you are investigating.

▶ **Predict**
Guess what will happen before you experiment.

▶ **A fair test**
If you are comparing how stuff behaves, make sure you keep everything the same in your tests except for one thing – such as the temperature or the amount of water.

▶ **Science notebook**
You will need a science notebook in which to put information about your investigations.

▶ **Record**
Write down what happened and perhaps make a drawing in your science notebook. You could take photographs too or make a video using a camcorder or mobile phone.

▶ **Make a conclusion**
Compare what happened with your prediction and see if you were right. It does not matter if you were wrong because it helps you rethink your ideas.

▶ **Experiments and answers**
Follow the steps in the experiments carefully. Use your science skills. There may be extra experiments and a question for you to try. Check all your observations, ideas and answers on pages 28–29.

▶ **What went wrong?**
Science experiments are famous for going wrong – sometimes. If your experiment does not seem to work, look for this section to help you make it right.

Cool crystals

The stuff inside the Earth is made from hot minerals. When they cool, they form crystals. Usually the crystals are so tightly packed you cannot see their shape. But sometimes, where there is a space, the mineral crystals grow without touching. They make beautiful shapes with smooth flat sides and pointed corners and ends.

▼ Granite is a rock made from crystals of mica (black), feldspar (pink) and quartz (white). They are all packed tightly together.

▼ These crystals have been magnified because they are usually too small to see. They were formed when hot metal cooled down.

► A geode is a piece of rock with a cavity in it. When it is cut open you can see the mineral crystals inside.

Getting going

You can find crystals in your own home! Sugar and salt have a crystalline form, but you need to use a magnifying glass to see these well. Epsom salts can be bought from a pharmacy and have a crystalline form. What's great about Epsom salts is that you can grow some new crystals from them in a couple of hours. Practise using your magnifying glass, see photo A, then follow steps 1–3.

Observing and growing crystals

A

Science box

Sugar, sea salt, Epsom salts (you must wash hands thoroughly after handling Epsom salts), a black plastic tray, three clear plastic trays (like the ones used to package vegetables), a magnifying glass, a teaspoon, a tablespoon, a clear plastic cup, a paintbrush, warm water.

Pour out some sugar, sea salt and Epsom salts in separate piles. Use a magnifying glass to look at the crystals. Move the magnifying glass until you can see the crystals clearly.

1

Put four tablespoonfuls of warm water into the plastic cup on the black tray. Add a teaspoon of Epsom salts and stir it in. Look in the bottom to see if they have all dissolved. Keep adding and stirring until some crystals are left undissolved at the bottom of the cup.

2

Dip the paintbrush in the Epsom salts solution and paint the bottom of one clear tray. Leave it in a warm dry place and check it every half an hour for signs of crystals.

3

When the solution has dried (the water has evaporated), use your magnifying glass to look for crystals. You could hold up the tray to a light (but not the Sun) to see them more clearly.

▶ **Observe**
How were the sugar and salt crystals similar and different? When the Epsom salts crystals form on the tray, what shapes can you see?

▶ **Record**
Make a sketch of the crystals.

▶ **Extra experiments**
Repeat steps 1, 2 and 3 with salt and sugar. You may have to wait until the following day or longer for any signs of the salt and sugar appearing. If you hold up the salt crystals they may roll off the tray.

▶ **Think about it**
Why do crystals form from the liquid after a while?

Dissolving rock

When some stuff dissolves in water, it turns the water into an acid. When carbon dioxide dissolves in rainwater, it makes the raindrops acidic. The acid rain can dissolve limestone rock creating potholes and caves. As a cave gets larger its roof can collapse and when this happens a gorge is formed.

▼ This pothole was formed by a stream of acidic rainwater dissolving and entering the rock.

▲ The sides of this gorge were once the sides of a huge cave. Part of the cave ceiling has fallen down and is now under the water.

Getting going

It takes a long time for rainwater to dissolve rock, so real scientists try to study what happens more quickly by making models. In this next experiment you use sugar cubes instead of limestone, and water instead of acid rain.

1 Make the base of the 'mountain' from four rows of four sugar cubes on the plate. Add four more layers of cubes to complete the mountain.

Sugar pothole

Science box

80 sugar cubes, a plate, a ruler, a teaspoon, a jug of water.

2 Put the ruler under one side of the plate to tilt it.

3 Take a teaspoon of water and pour it over the top of the mountain. Repeat twice more then examine the top.

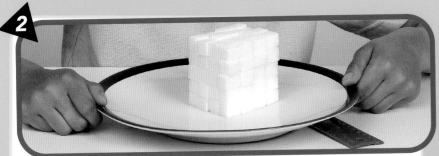

4 Find a place where the top has started to dissolve and pour more water onto it slowly. Look at the sides of the mountain and at other places on the top.

▶ **Observe**
What changes do you see in the sugar 'mountain' top as you begin to pour water on it?
What changes take place on the mountain as more water is poured onto it?
What happens to the water you pour onto the mountain?

▶ **Record**
Ask someone to film you as you pour the water onto the mountain top. They could move around the mountain as the water moves through it or set up the camera (make sure it is in focus) on the mountain and leave it running as you investigate.
Take a photograph every minute and arrange them in sequence in your notebook.

▶ **What's wrong?**
Doesn't form a pothole? Leave longer or add more water.

▶ **Think about it**
What happens to real limestone that dissolves in rainwater?

Inside a cave

When it rains in a limestone area the water seeps down into the rock. Rain dissolves limestone and, where there are caves underground, the water drips down from the ceiling to the cave floor.

At the places where the drops fall and then splash on to the cave floor, carbon dioxide leaves the water and tiny pieces of limestone stick together. These form stalactites on the ceiling and stalagmites on the floor. Over thousands of years the stalactites and stalagmites grow closer together until they touch and form a complete column of stone.

Getting going

As it takes so long for a stalactite and stalagmite to form you can make a model of the inside of a cave using a piece of woollen thread and a solution of baking soda instead of dissolved limestone.

1 Fill the cups three-quarters full with warm water and stir in baking soda into each of them until no more will dissolve.

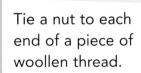

2 Tie a nut to each end of a piece of woollen thread.

10

Baking soda stalactite

▼ Some of these stalagmites and stalactites have joined together to form columns of stone.

Science box

Two plastic cups, baking soda, woollen thread, two metal nuts (or screws to weigh down the wool), a plastic tray (like the ones used to package vegetables), a spoon, warm water, and a place such as a windowsill where the experiment can be left for a few weeks.

3

Place the tray between the cups. Dip the ends of the thread into the baking soda solution in each cup. Let the thread hang down a little over the tray.

4

Look every day for a stalactite or stalagmite beginning to grow.

▶ Record
When the stalactite or stalagmite appears, draw their shape or take photographs. Measure the length of the stalactite every day and make a graph of the growth.

▶ What's wrong?
String won't start dripping? Dunk the whole piece of string in the solution and repeat 3–4.

▶ Think about it
Limestone rock is made from the fossil shells of sea creatures that lived millions of years ago. Will the stalactites and stalagmites have fossil shells in them?

▶ Extra experiment
Can you make a stalactite and stalagmite join together to make a column?

Gooey stuff

Gooey stuff is great fun because it is so unpredictable and has many uses. It helps to lubricate things, protect things and trap things because it has a high viscosity – it is thick and flows very slowly.

▼ Slime is a weird, slow moving material. It is produced by snails to help them move along and by some frogs to protect them from enemies – their slime is poisonous!

▲ The gooey stuff produced by the sundew plant is super sticky. It traps insects which the plant uses for food.

Getting going

The gooey stuff seen in nature is produced by chemicals and glands of animals and plants, but possibly the oddest gooey stuff is something that you might not see there – and you can make it yourself. It is a mixture of cornflour and water. Sometimes it acts like a liquid and at other times it behaves like a solid. Try making it for a weird, gooey experience – see A.

Goo and slime

Put two tablespoons of cornflour in a cup and add five tablespoons of water. Mix them together and pour the goo on your hands.

Now make some slime. Mix three tablespoons of flour with one-and-a-half tablespoons of salt.

Science box

Cornflour, two clear plastic cups, cold water, a bowl, wheat flour, salt, cooking oil, food colouring, a tablespoon.

2

Add one tablespoon of cooking oil and five tablespoons of water.

3

Mix a few drops of food colouring into the slime and stir well.

▶ Observe
Goo: squash the cornflour goo in your hand then release it. Smack the cornflour goo in your hand. Slime: put some of the slime on a spoon then tip the spoon to let it spill over the side. What happens?

▶ What's wrong?
Cornflour goo not changing? Squash harder!

▶ Predict and test
Split the slime into four pieces. Predict what would happen if you added more water, oil, salt or flour to each of the pieces then test your ideas.

▶ What's wrong?
No changes? Add more of the ingredient you are testing.

▶ Record
Ask someone to film you handling the cornflour goo and letting the slime slide off the spoon so you can make more detailed observations later.

▶ Think about it
The tiny pieces of cornflour have jagged edges but they can flow over each other if the water is not squashed. When the water is squashed it moves from between the tiny pieces. What do you think happens then?

Plastic fantastic

We live in a world of plastic. Your toothbrush is made from plastic and pens have plastic cases. A skateboader's helmet is plastic and when you use a computer you type using plastic keys.

There are many kinds of plastic and each one is designed to do a particular job. PVC (polyvinyl chloride) is used to make building materials. Nylon can be used to make clothing.

▼ The wheels on this skateboard are made of tough plastic called polyurethane. It can stand up to the wear of rolling over rough concrete surfaces.

▲ These are hot plastic fibres. Oil is heated and changed into gases, which are mixed with other stuff to make plastic.

Getting going
There is one kind of plastic that you can make without using oil. You just need milk and vinegar. The plastic is called casein.

Milk plastic

Pour warm water into the bowl and half fill the cup with milk. Put the cup in the bowl of water to warm up.

Science box

Warm water, a bowl, a plastic cup, milk, vinegar, a sieve, a tablespoon, a plate.

Add a tablespoon of vinegar to the warm milk and stir. Leave for five minutes and stir again.

Pour the milk and vinegar mixture into a sieve and let the water collect in the bowl below.

Scrape out the white solid from the sieve and place it on a plate. Make it into a disc and leave for a few days.

▶ **Observe**
How does the milk change when the vinegar is added? How does the white solid change after one day, two days and three days?

▶ **Fair test**
Make the plastic with very warm milk, then again with cooler water. Do you get the same result?

▶ **What's wrong?**
Cup floating and turning over in the bowl? Too much warm water – take some out.

▶ **Make a real scientist badge**
You could paint the disc with your name and make a *Real Scientist* badge by pushing a safety pin into it when it is wet. You could make some more plastic and make a warning sign for your home lab: *'Caution! Scientist at work!'*

Gusty gases

Gases are all around us in what we call 'air'. The gases do not have any colour so we can see right through them. As we move around, the gases flow over our bodies slowly and we do not feel them. But when the air moves quickly, as wind, we feel the gases straight away.

Air is made up of different gases called nitrogen, oxygen, carbon dioxide and water vapour.

▼ Air can move so fast that a strong gust can blow down a tree!

Getting going

We know that solids and liquids have weight – just pick up a stick or a glass of water – but what about air? There is a way to find out, but you have to be a very careful scientist.

1 Clip a paperclip to the neck of each balloon. Tape the clip (with the balloon!) to each end of the stick.

2 Tape the pencil to the top of the cereal packets. Place the stick on the pencil so that it balances. Mark the position on the stick where it pivots.

▼ Scuba divers take their supply of air with them – but do the tanks weigh more with or without air in?

Science box

Two balloons (the same size), a balloon pump, a long stick or cane about 45 cm (from garden centre), sticky tape, two paperclips, a pen, two empty cereal packets, a pencil.

3 Remove one balloon and inflate it with a balloon pump. When it is inflated, twist the neck and put the paperclip across it to prevent air escaping.

4 Replace the inflated balloon on the stick and use the pivot mark to put it back in the same place on the pencil.

▶ **Observe**
What happens when you try to balance the inflated balloon with the empty balloon? Inflate the second balloon to the same size as the first balloon and see if the two balloons can balance. What happens when you blow on them?

▶ **What's wrong?**
Difficulty getting the empty balloons to balance? Make sure you use the same amount of tape for each balloon. Make sure each balloon is at the end of the stick.

▶ **Record**
Ask someone to film you carrying out this test as you make the empty balloons balance.

▶ **Think about it**
What happens to the weight of a bicycle tyre as more air is pumped into it?

Brilliant bubbles

Water behaves as if it has a skin on it. Real scientists call this 'surface tension'. Water in a raindrop pulls on its surface to make it the least stretchy shape. This shape is a ball, and is why raindrops have a round shape.

When washing-up liquid and water are mixed together the stuff in the mixture pulls more weakly on the surface. This is why if you blow into the mixture some of it separates and forms a thin film, trapping air inside. The stuff in the film pulls on it to make the least stretchy shape, forming a ball around the air – a bubble.

▼ **These water droplets form a round shape because of surface tension.**

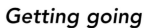

Getting going
Look at raindrops on the window when it rains. Watch how the droplets gather and then suddenly run when the surface tension is broken.

18

1

Half fill a plastic cup with water. Put two tablespoons of washing-up liquid into the water and stir.

2

Pour the bubble mixture into the tray. Make a small wire loop about 3 cm in diameter.

Science box

A plastic cup, water, a tablespoon, a piece of wire, washing-up liquid, a shallow tray (like the ones used to package vegetables), a straw.

3

Now dip the bottom of the plastic cup in the bubble mixture and place it upside down in the tray. Use the wire loop to blow a bubble and then gently place it on the bottom of the cup.

▶ **What's wrong?**
Can't blow bubbles on wire easily? Make up some more bubble mixture and leave it for a day before you use it.

▶ **Fair test**
Compare how freshly made and one-day old bubble mixture behave when you put a wire in them and use them to blow bubbles.

▶ **Observe**
What happens when you blow a bubble in a bubble?

▶ **Record**
Ask someone to film you blowing bubbles.

▶ **Think about it**
What happens if you make a larger loop? Try making an irregular wire shape. Can you still blow bubbles?

4

Get some more bubble mixture on the end of the straw and push the straw into the bubble. Blow another bubble inside it.

Violent stuff

Some of the most violent exploding stuff on Earth comes from an erupting volcano. Molten rock, called magma, is forced upwards from deep underground until it breaks through.

On the surface the molten rock is called lava. Often it shoots into the sky and slowly flows down the sides of the volcano cone. Gases in the magma below create super-heated bubbles that expand so quickly that they can cause explosions – flinging rock, called volcanic bombs, high into the sky!

▼ Molten rock explodes on to the surface in a fantastic volcanic eruption. After the eruption the molten rock will cool and harden.

Getting going

When some stuff is mixed together a violent reaction can take place. This happens because the stuff in the mixture forms new substances quickly, and one of these new substances is a gas. The gas bubbles up in the mixture and makes it spill out of its container. We can make a cola fountain just by using diet cola and Mentos. Watch out – they react violently together!

Open the bottle of diet cola and place it in a bowl.

Science box

500 ml bottle of diet cola, a packet of Mentos (or other softmint sweets), a narrow tube, a strip of card, a bowl.

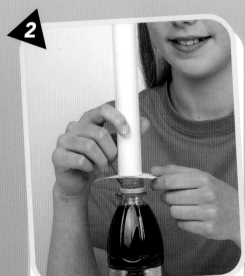

Place the strip of card over one end of the tube and lower on to the bottle. Slide five or six Mentos into the top of the tube.

Pull the strip of paper away so that the sweets fall into the bottle and move the tube away quickly. Sit well back!

▶ **Observe**
A Time how long the fountain lasts.
B Measure the height of the cola fountain.

▶ **Predict and test**
What will happen if you use a larger bottle of diet cola and more Mentos? Test your prediction outside!

▶ **Record**
Ask a friend to film you as you drop the sweets into the cola bottle.

▶ **Think about it**
Lava is molten rock – a liquid – but as it cools it turns into a solid. What's the name of this process? What other materials do this?

Flame reaction

When some stuff gets hot it takes part in a reaction with oxygen in the air and starts to burn. When most substances burn, energy is released in the form of heat, light and sound as the fire starts.

We use some stuff, such as wood on a campfire, as fuel. When fuels burn they release a lot of heat. Today large amounts of coal, oil and gas are burned in power stations to provide energy to generate electricity.

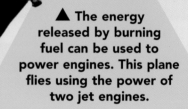

▲ The energy released by burning fuel can be used to power engines. This plane flies using the power of two jet engines.

▲ Fire, such as this campfire, needs oxygen, heat and fuel to burn.

Getting going

Fire can also be very dangerous so we are going to investigate a form of burning where flames are not made. When lemon juice is put on to paper the citric acid in it makes the paper weaker. When it gets warm it burns a little without actually making a flame. We can use it as an invisible ink to write hidden messages. All that is needed is some heat to make the message appear on the paper.

Invisible ink

Science box

A lemon cut in half, a juicer, a small paintbrush, a reading lamp, paper, an orange cut in half, apple juice.

1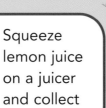

Squeeze lemon juice on a juicer and collect the juice.

2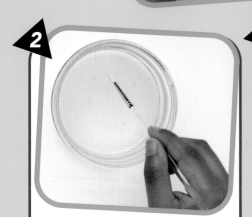

Dip the brush in the lemon juice and write a message with it on the paper. Leave the paper to dry.

3

Ask an adult to watch as you bring the paper near to the lamp.

4

Take the paper away from the lamp when the letters appear. The hidden message has been revealed!

▶ **Observe**
Can you see the message when the ink is dry? What happened when you brought the paper near the lamp?

▶ **Predict and test**
What might happen if you diluted the lemon juice with water? Test your prediction.

▶ **Fair test**
Try the experiment with orange juice and compare it with lemon juice.
Try the experiment with apple juice and compare it with orange and lemon juice.

▶ **Record**
Keep the copies of your messages in your science notebook.

▶ **Think about it**
Why should you stop heating the paper as soon as you can see the message?

Recycling stuff

We use tons of stuff during our lives – just think about all the empty cans and cartons you throw away each week. Most of this stuff comes from our surroundings – our environment. Plastic comes from oil, metals are found in rocks, and we use fuels from the earth.

We can recycle stuff so that less rubbish goes into landfill and less energy is used to make things. Scientists all over the world have helped to develop new technology that makes recycling possible.

▼ Wood is used to make different types of paper. These huge reels of paper will be used to make printer paper.

Getting going

Paper is made from wood and huge areas of forest are cut down every year to meet our needs. Paper can be recycled by mashing it up with water and other stuff to clean it up. In this investigation the paper is mashed up with plain, warm water to see if some more useful stuff can be made.

1 Tear up sheets of scrap paper into small pieces and mix together in a bowl of warm water to make a mash.

2 Pour the mash through a sieve and push down to get the water out. Scrape out the mash and spread it on a board.

Recycling paper

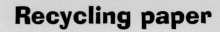

Science box

Eight or nine sheets of scrap printer paper, two bowls, a chopping board, a sieve, a rolling pin, warm water, a pen, a paintbrush.

▲ **Other stuff, including plastic, can be recycled or reused.**

3

Roll the sheet with a rolling pin then leave it in a warm place to dry. Carefully peel the paper off the board after a day.

▶ **Fair test**
Compare your paper with other kinds of paper. What is the same, what is different?
Write on your paper with a pen and a paintbrush. Which gives the best result?
Make some paper from old newspaper and compare it with the paper made from scrap printer paper. Try adding flour to the mash.

▶ **Record**
Keep pieces of your paper in your science notebook.

▶ **Think about it**
Why should you put out recycling for collection or take glass to the bottle bank?

What is stuff?

What is stuff really made of? In the late fifth century BCE, the ancient Greek, Democritus, came up with an idea. He thought if you cut up some stuff into the smallest pieces possible you would find a piece that was too small to cut. He called this tiny piece an atom.

Scientists eventually proved him right. There are over a hundred different kinds of atom and they can join together to make groups called molecules.

▲ In a solid, atoms and molecules are held firm.

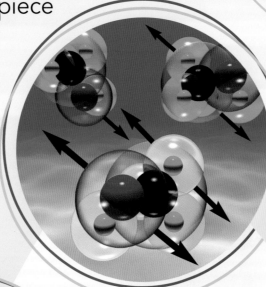

◄ In a liquid, atoms and molecules slide over each other.

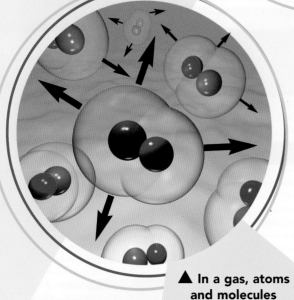

▲ In a gas, atoms and molecules move freely.

Getting going

Atoms and molecules are the matter that gives stuff its weight and density. Density is a measure of the amount of matter in a volume of stuff. We can compare densities quite easily, first by pouring liquids on to each other and then putting solids in the liquids to see where they go. The less dense liquids and solids float above the denser ones.

26

Comparing density

1 Pour syrup into the bottom of the vase.

2  Hold a spoon inside the vase. Pour the water onto the spoon and let it overflow. This will stop the water and syrup from accidentally mixing up.

▶ **Predict and test**
Predict where each object may go in the container before you carefully put it in. Test other objects.

▶ **Observe**
Look carefully where each object settles in the container.

▶ **Fair test**
How could you perform a fair test to compare the stuff in a piece of apple with the stuff in a piece of modelling clay? Try your test.

▶ **Record**
Take photographs of all the objects in the liquids.

▶ **Extra investigation**
Put some rock salt into the oil and observe what happens. Try and explain what you see.

▶ **Think about it**
Floating party balloons are filled with a gas called helium. Why do they rise up in the air?

3  Place the spoon above the water and pour oil on to the spoon as before.

4  Drop an object in the vase and record where it settles.

Results and answers

Page 7 Cool crystals

There will be more cubic crystals in the salt sample than in the other two samples. When the Epsom salts form crystals on the tray they are long and thin like needles packed tightly together and sometimes forming a fan. Sugar may form a layer rather than crystals when the water evaporates. Salt may form cubes but it may form a layer like sugar. The crystals form because the stuff they are made from cannot evaporate with the water.

Page 9 Dissolving rocks

Parts of the top dissolve straight away. Some parts near the cracks dissolve more than other places. The pothole in the crack gets bigger and caves may form in the sides. Eventually parts of the top may collapse and form gorges. The water flows away, like a river. On a real mountain the water carries away the dissolved limestone in streams and rivers to the sea.

Page 11 Baking soda stalactite

The stalactite is widest at the woollen thread and narrowest at its tip. It could reach four or more centimetres in length. The stalagmite will usually grow much later than the stalactite but may not grow at all. The fossil shells will not be present because they broke up as the limestone in them dissolved.

Page 13 Goo and slime

The cornflour goo will go solid when you squash it and then turn into a liquid when you let it go. It will go solid when you smack it. The slime should very slowly fall off the spoon. Extra water makes it runny. Extra oil makes it more slippery. Extra salt makes it less runny and extra flour makes it lumpy. The jagged edges of the tiny pieces in the cornflour lock together and make the mixture behave like a solid.

Page 15 Milk plastic

The milk forms solid lumps with the vinegar. The lumps stick together and form a larger lump which becomes harder and more yellow. Fewer lumps are made with cooler water and the lumps form more quickly and stick together faster with very warm water as heat speeds up the reaction.

Page 17 Weighing air

The scuba diver's air tanks weigh more with air in! The end of the stick with the inflated balloon goes down when you try and balance the balloons. The two inflated balloons should balance. When you blow on the balancing balloons you disturb the air, causing them to unbalance. Just like the scuba divers' air tanks, the weight of the bicycle tyre increases.

Page 19 Making bubbles

The mixture used straight away will be less successful because the mixture strengthens when it is left for a day. When you blow a bubble in a bubble it may attach itself to the bottom of the cup or it may form a half bubble in the side of the first one. A larger wire loop can make larger bubbles. Wires with irregular shapes still make circular bubbles as surface tension pulls the watery stuff into the least stretchy shape – a ball.

Page 21 Diet cola fountain

The eruption will start very quickly and may last for several seconds. The height of the cola fountain will depend on how many Mentos are used. The reaction will be more violent if a larger bottle of diet cola is used – and it is recommended that this is done outside. When volcanic lava turns into a solid, it does what every liquid does – it freezes. The rock freezes because its temperature goes below its freezing point. The freezing point of water is 0°C and nearly everyone thinks that is the only temperature stuff can freeze at. Rocks freeze at a few hundred degrees Celsius and gases, such as oxygen, freeze below minus 150°C.

Page 23 Invisible ink

The message cannot be seen when the ink is dry. It appeared as pale brown writing when the paper was brought near the lamp. The lime, orange and apple juices produced similar results to the lemon juice. If the paper got too hot it could catch fire.

Page 25 Recycling paper

Your recycled paper may tear the most easily if it is thin but may tear less easily if it is thicker. You will probably not be able to write as well on your paper as other paper. Recycled newspaper may be weaker than the recycled scrap printer paper. You should put out your recycling for collection because by recycling materials you are helping to conserve natural resources and reducing the impact that mining, logging, etc has on the environment.

Page 27 Comparing density

The liquids settle out in the following way starting from the top: oil, water, syrup. The wooden object and plastic brick float in the oil on top of the water. The coin settles on top of the syrup but slowly sinks into it. You can make a fair test by making the piece of apple and the piece of modelling clay the same size. In the extra investigation the rock salt sinks through the oil and takes oil drops with it into the water. The salt dissolves in the water and the oil drops rise back into the oil layer. Helium is less dense than air so it rises. At the top of the layer of air around the Earth there is a layer made up of hydrogen and helium. They are less dense than air so float on top of it.

Further information

Look at these websites for more information on materials and how they change:

▶ *http://www.bbc.co.uk/norfolk/kids/ science_experiments/slime/slime_01.shtml* This website shows you how to make a slime ball step-by-step with clear photographs and provides you with a hint to keep your slime from drying out!

▶ *http://www.goodearthgraphics.com/ virtcave/staltite/staltite.html* Look at some stunning pictures of stalactites at this website and compare them with the one you have grown. Be sure to click onto the links of the soda straw and deflected stalactites.

▶ *http://www.nationalgeographic.com/ngkids/ trythis/trythis_air/heavyweight.html* There are seven experiments about air at this website using only very simple equipment.

▶ *http://en.wikipedia.org/wiki/Soap_bubble* Scroll down this webpage to 'Sample formulae' to find a selection of recipes for making bubble mixtures.

▶ *http://www.sci.sdsu.edu/volcano* View an animation of a volcanic eruption at this website.

▶ *http://nationalgeographic.co.uk/ngkids/ trythis/secretcodes/scrabbled_letters.html* Make a simple code at this website for secret messages. Make sure the person you are sending the message to has a decoder.

▶ *http://pbskids.org/zoom/activities/sci/ recyclingpaper.html* This website introduces the use of more stuff in paper-making – a filler (cornstarch). You can compare your results and observations with others at the end of the instructions. There is a link – Zoom into action: Conservation Guide – with lots of ideas to help the environment.

▶ *http://www.chemsoc.org/viselements/ pages/pertable_fla.htm* Look at how the atoms of the different kinds of stuff are set out in a table and move your cursor across the table to learn their names.

Every effort has been made by the Publishers to ensure that these websites contain no inappropriate or offensive material. However, because of the nature of the Internet, it is impossible to guarantee that the contents of these sites will not be altered. We strongly advise that Internet access is supervised by a responsible adult.

Glossary

Atoms
Very tiny particles that make up all materials.

Carbon dioxide
A gas produced when animals breathe or substances burn which makes water slightly acidic.

Casein
A plastic made from milk.

Citric acid
An acid that is present in some fruit such as oranges and lemons.

Crystalline
Having the appearance of a crystal.

Density
A measure of the amount of matter in a certain volume of substance.

Dissolves
Breaking up into such tiny particles in water that it can spread out and not be seen.

Helium
A gas found in large amounts on the Sun and in very small amounts in Earth's atmosphere.

Hydrogen
A gas found in large amounts on the Sun and in very small amounts in Earth's atmosphere. It is the least dense of all materials.

Limestone
A hard, chalky rock.

Lubricate
To put a material (gooey stuff) on something to help it move.

Matter
The stuff that everything is made from. It is composed of atoms and molecules.

Minerals
Solid substances that form in the Earth. They can join together to form rocks.

Molecules
A group of atoms joined together.

Pivot
The place where one object makes a turning movement on another.

Predict
Say what will happen next after thinking about the experiment you are about to make.

Solution
A liquid in which other substances are dissolved.

Surface tension
The pulling forces of the molecules in a liquid on each other that make the surface appear as if it has a skin.

Temperature
A measure of the amount of heat in a substance.

Viscosity
A measure of the way a liquid moves when allowed to flow. A liquid of high viscosity flows slowly. A liquid of low viscosity flows quickly.

Volume
The amount of space taken up by a quantity of stuff.

Index

To my granddaughter
Pippa May

First published in 2008 by
Franklin Watts
338 Euston Road
London NW1 3BH

Franklin Watts Australia
Level 17/207 Kent Street
Sydney NSW 2000

Text © Peter Riley 2008
Design and Concept © Franklin Watts 2008

All rights reserved.

Series editor: Adrian Cole
Art Director: Jonathan Hair
Design: Matthew Lilly
Picture Research: Diana Morris
Photography: Andy Crawford (unless
otherwise credited)

Acknowledgements:
4uphoto/ Shutterstock: front cover br.
Afaizal/Shutterstock: 1,2br, 14. Joellen L
Armstrong/Shutterstock: front cover cr. Stefan
Ataman/Shutterstock: front cover ct. Bernard
Edmaier/Look/Alamy: 20. Noah Elhardt: 12cl.
Kuliyev Emin/Shutterstock: 18tr. Eye of
Science/SPL: 2ct, 6b. Laurence Gough/
Shutterstock: 2tl, 5t. Matthew Gough/
Shutterstock: 6cr. Peter Hansen/Shutterstock:
5b. Angela Hampton/Alamy: 3cr, 25tl. Robert
Harding PL/Alamy: 8l. Christopher
Howes/Wild Places/Alamy: 2cr, 8r. Russell
Kightley/SPL: 3bl, 26t, 26cl, 26cr. Andrey
Konovalikov/Shutterstock: 6tr. Karin
Lau/Shutterstock: front cover cl. Semen
Lixodeev/Shutterstock: 24-25c. Renata
Osinka/Shutterstock: 3tr, 18bl. Photobar/
Shutterstock: 16-17. Valery Potapova/
Shutterstock: front cover ctl. Elisei
Shafer/Shutterstock: 17tl. Ben Smith/
Shutterstock: 12. Gina Smith/ Shutterstock:
front cover bl. Charles Taylor/Shutterstock:
front cover ctr. David V./Shutterstock: 10-11.
Danny Warren/ Shutterstock: 3c, 22bl. A.T.
Willett/Alamy: 22tr. Serg Zastavkin/
Shutterstock: 4.
Every attempt has been made to clear
copyright. Should there be any inadvertent
omission please apply
to the publisher for rectification.

A CIP catalogue record for this
book is available from the
British Library.

Dewey number: 530.4

ISBN: 978 0 7496 7873 9

Printed in China

Franklin Watts is a division of
Hachette Children's Books,
an Hachette Livre UK company.
www.hachettelivre.co.uk